I Thought I Pulled Up My BIG Girl Panties but Apparently They Fell Down

Beth Ann Stockton

Preface

In 2016 I lost the most important person in
my life. My twin sister Jennifer. I could not believe
she was gone. I felt empty and alone. One day I
was trying to figure out my life and my future and
these words came over me.

Unless You Are Fearless Nothing Will
Change

I also told myself I needed to pull myself back
together. So, I thought I pulled up my big girl
panties but apparently, they fell down was started.

I knew I needed to get stronger, live with more
courage and be brave.

I also knew that Life can be hard so laugh a
little while you are in your storms. We all go
through different stages in life and learn different
lessons. So enjoy my stories and I hope you pull
your big girl panties up and live life.

The Lessons Of

Life

Love & Marriage Panties

Motherhood Panties

Be You

Faith

The Balancing Act

I Had My Big Girl Panties Up the Whole Time

Life

Welcome to the lessons of life!

The first rule to remember is. You will always be learning lessons in life. If you are not learning, you are not growing! So many lessons we learn along the way. In so many lessons we learn along the way.

In the 80's I think we all learned a lesson or two about our choice of hairstyle or the type of music we listened to. Those were some crazy times. If you look at styles today, every generation has their own style. It seems like the 80's and 90's are coming back in style.

If you were a teenager or maybe a parent to a teenager, you might have questioned the hair style or the type of music that was played. Who were the flock of seagulls anyway? The lessons we learn are from the choices we make every day. Some paths take us down roads we did not expect.

I know as a young girl I was faced with many choices. Jennifer, my twin sister, was one of my greatest lessons of all. She was my twin sister. She was strong and brave and lived beyond what the doctors told my parents. Her life had purpose.

One of the most important reasons was to show others how to love! She lived to show others to live and not waste one minute of their day on earth. She lived to show others how to love unfailingly, unwaveringly and with compassion and it was all God's plan! She was born with the umbilical cord around her neck cutting off the oxygen to her brain.

In results to this stressful entrance to life she was born mentally and physically handicap and soon after her birth they discovered she was blind too. She was born with no chance for a normal life. She was told by doctors she would never walk, communicate, or show any kind of progress or growth.

But she proved us all wrong and she did so much more. She taught me to see. She showed me how to see others. I learned the difference between living for me and living for others. She walked with me through the storms of life. Having her by my side showed me to embrace life and be fearless! She helped me discover that I am unique and that my soul has purpose. She did this through her smile and her laughter and her determination to never give up.

In life we only get a few chances to be real and to live a fearless life. Jennifer was a human being that communicated through love and through her soul. She spoke volumes, by hardly speaking at all.

Her soul was an instrument and was used to change the hearts and minds of so many people. She loved more people through her voice and her smile than I will ever do. Her life meant more to me than I can put into words.

I am confident because she showed me to accept myself for who I am, not what I am trying to become. She struggled through her disabilities but never gave up.

She did not understand the concept of judgement. The simple act of her smile showed me to love without judgement. Even though her eyes were open, all she saw was darkness. She was blind, but she taught me to see. The ability to live a life and learn not to judge. To be fearless, love others, have kindness, have an unwavering heart and an unfailing Christ driven life. These are lessons of life learned at a young age. Thank you, Jennifer,

I promise I will never forget you.

November 2016

You were and still are my superhero.

~ 9 ~

We learn a lot about life through the trials and storms that come our way. If we are lucky and blessed to have people by our side and telling us the truth about life and relationships and being honest with our feelings even if it hurts. Truth and integrity are what relationships build on and it is what carries us through the lessons of life.

The lessons I learned from a little girl helped me as I got older, but nothing can prepare you for life. You do not know when, how and why storms come our way. As you go through the different seasons of life the lessons change, you change and so do your relationships. I know writing this book as a wife, mom, and businesswoman I have had many seasons of changes and some I embraced and others I cried through asking why this, why now? So sometimes you must pull up your big girl panties and keep moving, keep living and keep believing.

I wrote the book Live Like It Matters and Love Like Crazy back in 2014 and a second edition in 2024.

The reason I wrote it was solely on life and the love my twin sister showed me. So, when she passed away, I felt so empty and alone. I had no desire to move forward. How could I with my other half gone. It was not until 2017 I was standing in my living room saying "What next God? Where do I go from here." I heard God say, "Unless You Are Fearless Nothing Will Change!"

I pondered on those words for a few. I said "OK, I will be Fearless in everything I do." I might fail, that is ok. I might fall and surly I knew I would, but that is ok.

So, as I began to reflect on those words, I concluded that I needed to pull up my big girl panties and get to work. I needed to keep living for me. This is where I started writing this book.

I wanted to write about the lessons of life. Because if we are not learning we are not growing. I thought I pulled up my big girl panties but apparently, they fell down was started. My sister's life and her mission would always stay close to me. I have written poetry since I was 15 and have a poetry book published called Life Speaks Truth and so when it came time for my sister's funeral, I knew I had to speak on her behave. I wrote a poem and read it at her funeral and these words might not hold importance to you but, these words are my soul, and this is what she meant to our family.

I spoke at the funeral as if my sister could say one last thing to her family and friends and these are the words that came to my heart.

To my mom, Mom thank you for your voice, you spoke for me when no one else could. You sang to me like an angel would. You made me feel beautiful every single day. The strength of a warrior entering into battle, you fought for my life and never did you settle.

To my dad, Dad thank you for being my feet, and carrying me through life with everyone you meet. Your words of wisdom were always around, and you taught me to never give up even when I was down.

To my brother Mark, thank you for being my protector, and watching over me. Thank you for always being strong for our family. Your humor and laughter kept our family alive and through that we all thrive.

P.S. Thanks for not being so hard on that twin sister of mine; we know she can be a bit sensitive."

I then shared a second poem that I wrote in memory of my twin sister Jennifer.

Dear Sister, oh, how I miss you so. You left too soon. I will keep looking for you.

I keep thinking you are here, but every time I turn around, I find myself in tears.

I turned the lights on, but it is still so dark. show me a sign, don't let me stray, hold my hand, and show me the way.

You are a part of me, and I am a part of you. You gave me hope no one else could do.

You helped me believe my life has purpose and my life has meaning, to never give up and to keep on dreaming.

It is I who was blind and could not see for all along you were the one leading me.

Reach out and don't let go for I need you now more than ever before.

Dear sister, walk with me and stay by my side, show me that our friendship will never die.

I thank God for the miracle of your life and the time we had, I promise I will try not to be too sad.

I will cherish your smile and what it meant to me, I will live my life with purpose and meaning.

Dear sister, I won't let you down.

I love you, your other half.

Beth Ann Stockton

Life's lessons can be complicated and confusing.

Everyday struggle is real. One day you think you got this thing called life, then the next day you have a meltdown.

You're throwing a tantrum like your 2-year-old does or maybe like your 12-year-old. Either way you are in a battle with yourself. Your tantrum is over the chores, yes, the chores that you did not get done or the frustration of your teenager and the choices they make. Maybe your tantrum is over something much bigger than these examples. Life can throw a lot at us and most of the time we were not expecting it. We did not even see it coming. From the small frustrations and trials to the big life happens.

You ran out of milk for the millionth time, and you were just at the store. Your boss needs those reports by the end of the day. Your kids need to be at a game, and it is your turn for snacks. Your son can't find his gloves!

Your daughter does not like the way her hair looks and it's all your fault. What will you cook for dinner? You have family, work, and life issues every day. Forget about painting your toenails. The gross chipped-nail polish look is in style these days.

We are WWAM.

Worn out Women and Moms.

Meltdowns are ok and are needed every so often. It gets out the frustrations of life. Your big girl panties have not fallen down, they are merely in intermission.

The chores will get done sometime this century. To solve the milk problem, you might have to invest in a cow, they are only a couple thousand dollars. If you are your own boss, or you work for someone, remember God is in control.

The seasons of life can be long and seem to be muddy sometimes, but life is short so take a deep breath. The sun will come out tomorrow for sure.

Hug your children a lot, tell them you are proud of them. For you want them to grow up not go away! Don't try to be perfect at everything.

If you spend your whole life trying to be perfect or live the perfect life, I can guarantee you will not succeed. Life can not be perfect, for we make mistakes to learn, to grow and to rely on Christ during the storms.

Sometimes just let the milk run out. Let the chores go. Let your tantrums be hilarious. Be honest with yourself and your spouse. It will all be ok.

If you're going to live,

Live life with your Gig Girl Panties up!

Love and Marriage Panties

Stories that can make you sit back and say, "amen sister!" Lessons that make you feel like you're not alone in this crazy world of marriage. Marriage is like waiting for a sloth to win a marathon. It takes a long time and a lot of hard work. I remember my first year of marriage. I was so proud of myself for cooking a great spaghetti dinner for me and my husband. I had everything for a great meal. I had the sauce, the meat, and the noodles.

Now all that was left was for my husband to come home. When my husband came home, he said, "Something Smells great." I said, "I cooked spaghetti!" Now as a new wife I guess the expectation of good cooking might have been there, but that is one thing I did not learn how to do well, and that is cook. You would not die if I cooked for you but there are no gold stars coming my way. He was excited to eat after a long day at work.

I made our plates and he looked at the plate and looked at me disappointedly and said, "Where is the sauce?" I made so many noodles and mixed the meat and sauce together and put it on top of the noodles. There were way more noodles than sauce. As I looked at him with eyes of like that is the first words you are going to say, I wanted to dump the spaghetti on his head. I just walked away and cried. Now I am a sensitive person and I know he did not mean it the way it sounded, but he comes from a real Italian family so my Ragu spaghetti sauce was not looking so good. Looking back, it would have felt good to dump it on his head.

At least we could have laughed years later. I mean come on a newly married wife has some grounds for this kind of thing, right? It is still a funny joke to this day. I have learned how to make great meals over the years. I am not the best cook by far, but at least we eat!

Lessons about love and marriage can teach us a lot about ourselves. I have learned a lot about myself. Take this for instance. My brain must work through being a mom, wife, woman, and my career and my relationship with God. Our brain can give 100% energy most of the time, well maybe until 9 or 10 at night depending on the day.

The way it is divided is another story. The divided brain. I became a mom at 27. I was married for a good 4 years before that journey started. I had so much time before that to figure out who I was and who I wanted to be. I spent the ages of 23-26 trying to work and figure out who I was. Lost is what I was. Although I was working, I was not really taking any chances with life. I could have done so much during this time, and I did not.

I don't know if I was afraid or just living in the shadow of thinking I am just not smart enough. Growing up takes time and takes life. I was expecting my life to be figured out before I became a wife or a mom, but that did not happen. It was during those many years that I grew and discovered who I wanted to be. Looking back, I was doing something, I was figuring out the dos and don'ts of life, and what I wanted out of life. I was finding my strengths and my weakness; I just did not realize it then.

Here I am in my 40's and life has thrown me a few punches. I have had my share of storms. It is through those trials that shape you, grow you. You are forced to make decisions when life does not go the way you had planned. In the decision to write this book, it was time for me to pick up my big girl panties and keep them up. I wanted to do so much but the energy was slowly depleting from my body.

Being a mom and wife really sucks you dry. I had to learn to put myself first more often than I did. I think that this is hard for a lot of people. It does not matter if you are a man, woman, mom, or a dad. Life gets busy and we are always moving and working and giving to others. We need time to relax and rejuvenate ourselves. I am ready to pull up my big girl panties and start seeing what I want out of life. When I was younger, I just went along with the crowd and didn't set my own boundaries or see what I wanted.

It was always thinking about others and what they wanted. I was afraid to have my own thoughts and opinions. I wanted to be liked and too scared to cause waves. I also had put all my focus on my kids and my marriage that I felt like I was needed. The truth is yes, I may have been needed especially when my kids were young, but the family would have been fine without me. Sometimes as moms we feel like the world will come to an end if we leave our home or take some rest and take care of ourselves. Everyone needs it, not just women and moms.

My fear was my kids will need me and I will not be there for them. My fear was my husband will want help and I won't be able to help. My fear is "what if I fail? Will I use the gifts God gave me?" Being a mom is the most important job of all. But if you are not sowing into yourself, then you cannot be there for anyone else.

I must put my fear in
the palms of my
hands
and squash it.

Love is a big word used in marriage, but what is the definition of love? We learn so much about ourselves from our spouse.

Marriage is saying I love you before you go to bed. You never want to go to bed upset.

I know I have a few times and man I am so thankful to be able to wake up and say I am sorry, or I love you!

In my 20's the panties were small, pretty, and fearless. I was Mary Poppins with tons of energy. I could do it all and still look good! I had tons of energy! In my 30's the panties were slowly worn out and not so pretty.

As a young mom and wife, I was starting to slow down a little. I had a lot of energy still. The house still got cleaned and the kids were taken care of, and I was able to maintain myself on the outside.

But I never saw it coming, that on the inside I was slowly going downhill, and those big girl panties were never going to make it up.

Pouring into your family takes a lot of energy.

If you have a deadline on a project and you were being graded on it, you will give 110% to that project. My husband and kids were my project every single day. When I was 37- or 38-years old Mary Poppins was not so Poppin or merry.

My fire for life slowed down. The energy level decreased, and Mary Poppins started to look like Mary Pooped. At 40, yeah it isn't happening!

Trying to keep it all together just does not work! but there is beauty in that. Here is the truth, if you really want to know, read carefully.

It's your Faith!

It's Trust!

It's Letting Go!

I know finding food in the pantry for your three kids is hard because you went grocery shopping on Monday, and it's gone by Tuesday. There is no end to cleaning, grocery shopping, loving, and giving to your marriage and to your family. Poppins, where did you go? Deep down in my soul I know you're still there.

Knowing you don't have to pull your big girl panties up because you are perfectly imperfect just the way you are.

Motherhood Panties

Living a life with a 4.0 PhD Personal Heart Degree. I am living life through my soul not my head. I have lived my life with the feelings hanging off my shoulders. It has not been easy being an overly sensitive person. Trying to play the role of what a good mother looks like is hard. There seems to be so much competition. Who raises their kids the best, who has the best home with perfect pictures on the wall.

I realize there is just not enough time for all that nonsense.

Are your kids loved?

Do they know Jesus?

Do they know forgiveness?

Do they know life is not perfect?

I am all that and a bag of chips!!

She says with an attitude!

If you look hard, you will see what I mean. I am all that and I ate the bag of chips too. I don't look the same in my 40's as I did in my 20's! My big girl panties are up but are they worn out or figured out?

It's not what you know.

It's not who you know.

It's who you serve!

These sayings and ideas are what our children hear from us every day! What will my children think about themselves. What image do they have in their heads. What leads them to the right choices. Keeping it real with our kids even if it hurts them or hurts us, keep the conversation real, keep an open mind to what they are feeling.

They will grow up knowing you listened to them not pushed the rules and obligations down their throats. You were more than an authoritative parent. You were relatable too.

KIR

KEEP IT REAL.

Keeping it real for our children today is vital to their future. Giving them the tools to use and lead them in the direction so they can make decisions on their own. Let them see your faults and failures and what you learned from it. Let them see that you are not perfect but that you are real. Take off the mask and be real. keep it real. Be honest in your marriage for your kids are watching you and learning from you.

If you feel something, don't hide it. Don't keep those feelings under the rug. Don't hide your fear, get it out. Don't hide any imperfections embrace them. Don't let the waves of life pull you down. Motherhood is so important. Keep it real with your kids. teach them about respect! Respect is a positive feeling or action shown towards someone or something considered important or held in high esteem or regard; it conveys a sense of admiration for good or valuable qualities.

Teach them to respect themselves and to respect others. With technology today, our children are being exposed to much more than their brains can handle. Violence, sex, drugs, perfection, anger, rage, racism, YOU DO YOU!! Meaning who cares what others think and don't hold yourself to must standards. What our kids see is that I don't have to do 100% and that I can get away with doing something halfway. No consequences for their actions. Teaching them to value their voices, their opinions, and their heart.

Tell them to value their body, mind, and soul. You can be the parent that has the rules and has limitations. If they don't see it and learn it from you, they will seek the world and we know where that is going. Be strong in your beliefs and in your convictions, live with integrity so they see this.

Rules for Motherhood

KEEP IT REAL.

BE HONEST

SAY YOUR SORRY

ADMIT YOUR NOT PERFECT

BE HUMBLE

HAVE GRACE

SING LOUD

HUG LONGER

HAVE EYE CONTACT

LISTEN BETTER

LOVE HARDER

BE THERE

BE THERE

BE THERE

REMEMBER YOU WERE A KID ONCE.

I love being a mom! I think it has taught me more about myself than anything else. You will fall and you will get hurt, the waves of life might take you under and the uncertainty that comes your way. But unless you try you will not know what you are capable of. Also, our kids are honest and will tell us the truth about our own actions. Our kids are like a mirror image in front of us. But if you pick yourself back up and believe you can then you will and by doing so you show your kids they can too.

Don't be afraid to be a parent to your kids and not just their friend. We struggle with that because we want that relationship with our kids to be good. But for it to be good it must be right and honest and built on truth. It also takes a lot of humility and listening to them. If you choose to put the friendship first and not the responsibilities that God has placed before you, then you're asking for trouble.

I remember a time my daughter was just throwing a fit and I was losing control of the situation. When we mothers get to the boiling point, we can lose it. I think this situation was to my advantage but sort of backfired on me.

My daughter was throwing a fit and her behavior was getting out of control and disrespectful. She was standing in our hallway one morning, throwing a fit. I looked at her and we were face to face and I spoke to her about her attitude and how it needed to change. She looked at me; mind you she was 3 or 4 years old.

She looked at me and said, "mom your breath is really bad." I looked at her but inside I was laughing. I said to her, "Well, this is part of your punishment to smell my morning bad breath!' It's something we laugh about now! But things were not always easy. I made mistakes as a mother. During my childhood there was not a lot of conflict and my parents worked to provide a great life for us but in the end, there was a lot hidden under the rug.

Life will happen and disagreements will arise, it is how you work through them, talk them out and be real. Putting on a front or saying you are ok when you are not ok will never allow you to grow as a person, or within your marriage and as a parent. When you are open to truth, you are saying I care enough even if you are mad, even if we fight. I did not see this as a child so as I got older, I did not know how to deal with conflict.

This can affect your marriage and of course affect you in parenting because you need to be able to hear your kids out especially when they don't even know how they feel themselves or how to process their own frustration. Setting boundaries within yourself will help you be a more attentive and a loving mother because your kids know where you stand and respect you for it. Remind yourself you do not have to be, nor will you be a perfect mom and your kids will not be perfect either, so set out for truth, honestly and maybe some tears and learning.

Motherhood is like going into battle!

You don't know when the enemy will attack,

but you know they are out there.

I have had to figure out these lessons of life and through it has not always been easy. It wanted to keep the peace in the home. I became a peace maker. Not only did this prevent my husband from taking charge at certain times that were needed, but I also metaled in the problems to keep the peace. This was my way of handling situations. It was not the right way to handle things and of course it affected my home, my kids, and my marriage. I am thankful that I married a man that is honest, and we could talk about truth and the reality of life.

What kind of person do you want to be? What do you want to stand for? What do you want to be remembered for? Your career? What does God have in store for my life? Where will I make the difference? What are my talents? Searching my soul, asking questions of what matters to me? What do I want to do in my life? What about me? My marriage?

What kind of wife do you want to be?

What kind of marriage do you want to have?

I have asked you a few questions, take a moment and read these questions again and write out your thoughts.

There is no perfect parent, wife, or woman.

But coffee does help!

What kind of mom do you want to be?

What kind of example do you want to show? leaving a legacy behind for your kids and their kids! Pull the panties up and live life!

You only got one life to live!

No, I am not talking about the soap opera on tv!

Be You

Why? Well because there is only one you!
Here are some reasons why I decided to be me! I
was living everyday trying to live up to this
expectation of what a real woman looked like. She
has her high heels on and dresses to the nine. She
uses big fancy words. She is smart and serious and
ready to attack the world.

I love wearing high heels and dressing
nicely. But what defines me? Smart, I would say I
am smart. Put me in a room full of doctors and I
am smart enough to know I am not capable of
performing the heart transplant.

What makes us different makes our world a better place. We all have our gifts and talents. I am a woman who wants to grow and change the world. It is not a one woman show! It takes all kinds of women coming together to change the world. I had this idea of what a woman looks like. What a woman, mom and wife had to be to fit the mold.

I thought that if I had that better job, then I would look the part. There is so much pressure to be everything. I told myself, I did not finish college, so what will I do with my life? I did not have all the answers at the age of 20. I did not know my future. I did not know what I wanted to be. I was still figuring me out. Looking back on my life, I would not change a thing. My path led me right where I belong.

I would often think about how I must become much more serious than I am if I want to fit this description of the woman with her big girl panties up.

But that is not true. I needed to be just how God made me to be. I was created for just such time as this. This is me,

I am loud!

I am silly!

My fancy grown up word is love.

I use my heart a lot more than my head.

Here is the real issue.

We are all different.

We need strong women from all walks of life out there who can rock it. I know I am a strong woman. I am Fearless! I know I am capable. I am also human. I thought I pulled my up my big girl panties, but apparently, they fell down. I keep trying and trying to pull them up. They are not moving in the direction I want them to go. Why, because I was pulling them up for all the wrong reasons.

Look in the mirror and see for yourself.

Who do you see?

Do you like what you see?

Trying to become someone you were not meant to be makes life harder. So let go of trying so hard and just be you. You are being you and me being me is what makes the world go round. When you realize God created you the way you are for a reason. If you try to change that, well expect a long rough road ahead. Expect disappointment and sadness. That is something I realized along this journey and in writing this book.

I was trying to pull up my big girl panties so high that I think I hurt myself physically. I would have them pulled up and I would hold them tight. I wanted so bad to be accepted as this woman. Who had it all going on? I wanted to appear perfect. I wanted to fit in this mold I made for myself, but the mold was not made for me.

So, I let go and I dropped my drawers. I know I will never be a CEO of a major company or become the next female neurosurgeon.

I know that I am capable of learning new things and growing as the woman I want to be, and the woman God made me to be.

So, say goodbye to the Big Girl Panties and say hello to the

Wonder Bra!

Just Kidding.

Say hello to me.

Over thinker

Sensitive

Loud

Crazy Courageous

Live life by my heart

My head may follow sometimes.

Passionate about music

Writer

Giver

Believer

Forgiven sinner

Lover of family

Mom

Small business owner

Animal lover

Silly

Relentless

I am just a woman trying to make it in this world
as a human being, woman, wife, mother, and
Believer.

**Life takes us through a journey, try to
remember never to be in a hurry. Life takes us
through unexpected places and many different
faces but as long as we show kindness.
I know love will find us.**

Faith

Faith is the complete trust or confidence in something or someone!!! I have faith that my big girl panties will stay up! How? I don't know!
I guess with a whole lot of faith and a little bit of duct tape!!! Or maybe a lot of duct tape!
Waking up with faith is so important to me.

I know that having faith in yourself is so important. If you don't have faith in yourself, who will? God does.

I know God created you to do great things, so believe in that. God wants you to believe in yourself because your faith is in him.

I am covering up my wrinkles and tucking in my fat!

In a different book that I wrote a few years back called Live Like It Matters and Love Like Crazy, in this book I talk about how our faith in God and believing in yourself is vital to your life. It is the source to truth and having a true relationship with God.

This book speaks truth about our lives. What does it mean to really live like that. Faith is something that you must put your trust in even if you cannot see it. We put our trust in government and money and other worldly things but from where I am standing it has not been a great thing to put our trust in. Faith is defined like this. Faith is having complete trust or confidence in someone or something. Faith is also having complete trust or confidence in God. I know for me, faith has been a growing seed inside me and the better I am at watering it, the better it grows. It is kind of funny how your faith can grow.

The changes that have happened in my life have come in all different ways. Growing as a woman, mom and wife do not happen all at once and some growing is way harder than you expected. It is in the storm you will see God; it is in the trials you will see healing, and it is in the healing you will grow.

I wanted to experience so many things in my life. I wanted to try it all. But God created each of us unique and differently, so I am who I was meant to be. I really wanted to be a dancer and a singer when I was a little girl, I think a lot of children have huge dreams when they are young. So, I wrote a small poem. Enjoy!!

I wish I could sing,

I wish I could dance.

Those are not the gifts

that God had planned.

God showed me my
talents to be used.

For with this gift, I will
not lose.

I thought I had to go to college to find myself. I have found myself and have dug deep into my soul to find the meaning of life. The secret to life is having faith, keep on dreaming, always love deeply. Grow within, laugh, smile and breath.

Having faith is not always easy. It means letting go and trusting God and others. Part of growing up is seeking faith within. There comes a moment in one's life when the light bulb turns on. You realize the person that God wants you to be is right in front of you. You must trust in yourself and believe in yourself. That person is you!

My Big Girl Panty journey started several years ago! I started to find me and my voice! When I started to discover more about who I was, the bigger the problem became. I was trying to spend time and energy on myself, and the demands of life were right under my feet all the time. I felt a pull away from my husband and kids.

A strong force to be alone came over me. My mom's world and wife's world changed. I started to lose my faith in myself and my purpose because I was not sure if I could do it all. It is hard to separate yourself from the role of motherhood and being a wife, but also taking care of yourself. I am sure men and fathers can have the same issue with finding themselves outside of their work and their children. It is different for everyone because like I said earlier everyone is different and has different roles in life.

As time went on, I could not stop the feeling of wanting more for myself. The feelings I needed of growth and life inside were growing bigger than I expected. As my faith and trust in God grew, I also started to grow. I began to understand my purpose! When you are blinded by the day to day and the ins and outs of life you turn off the life button and become a robot. You become what everyone else wants. Your soul dies. You are just a shell. Your vision becomes cloudy, and you feel like you are in hell. Don't let this happen to you.

Be set free from the worry and fear that this world lets you believe. In 2012 I started my own company called Pinky Got Purses. The start of Pinky was a start of so much more than I could have ever imagined. I had a purpose to make my business grow. As my purpose, and my thoughts and dreams started to fill my mind. I knew deep down I wanted to do more. I wanted to leave a legacy for my children. I wanted them to know my heart and that I was not perfect and that I fell down a lot but that I got myself back up.

So, this is when and where I stepped out in faith
and wrote,

LIVE LIKE IT MATTERS

AND

LOVE LIKE CRAZY.

I published it in 2015. This book gave me a new outlook on life, to live each day to the fullest. My twin sister inspired me. Her laugh, her smile, her heart lived within me.

I started to promote my book and hoping for my message and my mission to change people's hearts and minds. Little did I know it radically changed mine! As I mentioned earlier in this book,

November 2016 my sister suddenly passed away.

I will never forget where I was when I heard the news. I was devastated, but somehow my faith grew so much stronger. We cannot see, taste or smell faith. We can want it, crave it, seek it, but until we let go and let our faith grow us. We won't know what true faith is! Faith is the belief God created you and made you for a reason and a purpose.

The Balancing Act

I would say this has been the hardest part of my journey. It is also the most important one.

Balancing life is hard! Shortly after my sister died, I became extremely depressed. I missed her so much and felt like a piece of me died the day she died. I had so many questions. I thought she could finally see me, but I cannot see her.

I was so angry! I wanted to die myself just so I could see her. I know it sounds crazy but that is what I thought. The balancing act just became harder and more emotional. I was trying to balance my faith in God now that my sister was gone, balance who I am now that I am no longer a twin. My marriage and being committed to always working at it because that is what you do. Being a mother to three kids and I know I made some mistakes there but learned a lot too. Learning how to work and create a business with purpose and to grow it.

Writing was and is always on my mind. I wanted to conquer the world! It is a balancing act I was not always the best at. I was trying to do it all and be all I thought I could be. I had a few too many dreams and passions to balance them all at once. All of these were and are very important to me. Knowing how to balance them and keep them in the right order is the key to making it all worth it.

God,

Is the number one thing I needed and wanted in my life. Prayer became stronger for me when my sister died. I felt a connection to heaven. Learning to trust God and knowing I cannot do this thing called life on my own. It becomes too hard when you try to put God and your trust in him alongside the world and balancing that too. My faith literally became a balancing act between the world and God. I wanted what God wanted more than what the world wanted. Even though I strived for what God had in store for me, it did not always happen.

I still struggled with having one foot in and one foot out! I know God is bigger than my balancing act! He has me in his hands! Now that I had found my purpose and knew it would be a lifelong journey not a destination. I was finding my faith for what God wanted me to be, the balancing of it all needed to include diving into myself and God's word, my family and close friends.

I started to see through all my visions and dreams and thoughts that if I do not take care of me, there will be nothing left of me to be a writer, business owner or most importantly a wife and mom. But I ask myself how do I balance it all? Knowing you need yourself is the first step. It is important to take the time to be alone with yourself and be still. To listen to your heart and what it needs. Pay attention to your body. Not an easy thing to do when you are just going, going, and going. I let my health go in the wrong direction.

Don't let work or others steal your time or your joy. This is easy to do. I am a social person and I want to love everyone, so sometimes I come last. Take care of yourself and learn to balance your home, work, and family time. Learn from your mistakes. Grow in them, let them guide you to a stronger person. Don't look at the glass half empty but fill it up and empty out the mess and let in the good.

Marriage

These days this seems to be the first thing to go. We are quick to say; this is just not working out, let's get a divorce. When times get hard and the balancing act becomes too much, we give up on what we think it the problem, but the root is you.

Your marriage is not the root of the problem, it is the expectation you are putting on yourself and your spouse. In marriage you should talk about your love languages and your expectations you have on a regular basis and remind each other of these things so you can grow closer. It is the untold truth and the lack of communication that will drown you both. No spouse is perfect. expecting them to make you happy is unrealistic. It is too much for one person to carry. Let your marriage breathe. Let your marriage go through the growing pains. Give your marriage a chance. Give your spouse a break! Hug them more! Kiss passionately and go on dates.

Motherhood

I knew I always wanted to be a mom. I had no idea how many kids I would have or if I would have boys or girls. I was blessed with two boys and one girl. The balancing act for children and motherhood is, well let's just say it is a whole new balancing act of **crazy**! When you become a parent, people give you words of advice. I wish someone would have told me to do take it personally. Your kids will not like you someday even after all you do for them. Remember that at their birth and remind yourself that every day from that moment on.

Your kids are their own people and one day will leave and start their own life so start preparing now. You are responsible for this tiny person, and you do not know their future, but you need to realize it is their future not yours. Hard pill to swallow. I know from experience.

Knowing what is right for them and having that confidence in your decision. Breathe between fights. Laugh with them often. Build them up every chance you get and knowing when to walk away. Listen to them with the right intention and without correction all the time. Listen with humility. Kids look at adults like we are either disappointed in them or better than them and they should never feel either one of these things, that is why parenting is such an important balancing act.

It is like Tom Cruise in the Mission Impossible movies. You walk a fine line and one step wrong it will blow up in your face. If you teach your kids grace and forgiveness and they see your true heart, they will hopefully see you are real and that you make mistakes too, but it is important to learn how to be a parent not just call yourself one. Be present, be real, be forgiving and listen a lot.

I love being a mom, I also love to sleep, eat warm meals, hang out with my husband, and not clean any more dishes. You must balance between loving your kids and loving yourself and your spouse. Helping them each realize their strengths and weaknesses. Show them love and grace and more grace and show them you have faith. Show them Jesus. Also be patient with them. They might not agree with all your ways, showing they are individuals will help. Give them space to think for themselves and to grow. Share wisdom through stories and let them see you are human.

Remember to smile with them and go camping or go to the movies. Have popcorn fights and sleep overs. Balance the good and the bad with your kids. Build a relationship built on balance, love, grace, mercy, humility, and more love.

Fearless Enterprise

Pinky Got Purses has been my passion really my whole life. I loved purses as a little girl. I was always found in my grandma's closet playing with her purses and shoes. My grandma's name was Marilyn, but her nickname was pinky. That is where Pinky Got Purses is from. When I started Pinkys Got Purses, it just became so much fun. I had started something on my own. It grew into something bigger than I planned. I started writing during the beginning of Pinkys and it just grew. Becoming a writer was therapeutic for me. I released so many different thoughts, dreams, and ideas.

It became my outlet for what was going on inside. I also did marketing on the side for several different companies to bring in extra income. So, the balancing act for me was intense. I was stretching myself to thin.

There are so many days in a week and hours in a day to get everything done. I have my good days and my bad days. It all goes back to God. Putting him first in the decisions I make every day. It is asking for his wisdom and guidance in my week, my day, my hour or even my minute. Figuring out how to balance my career and my family is hard. I had to make choices, and this is where you must ask yourself am I going to pull up my big girl panties or if I let them fall, I will trip and that will not look pretty.

You can't do it all, all the time. something will fail. Someone will get left behind. Make sure your dreams and your feelings are communicated to your family. You want their support. Make sure the lines of communication are open. Remember it is ok to focus on yourself.

Just don't forget others love you and at the end of the day you will want to connect with people and family.

So, I am learning how to balance it all.

Me

Marriage

Mom of three

Business owner

Writer

and more.

The dishes will get cleaned or there are always paper plates. The laundry will grow, so just keep picking away at it. You might eat pancakes for dinner a few times. That is not so bad.

The key to the balancing act is. There is no key or magic button. Learning to balance your life with work, family and your personal time is an everyday process, and you must wake up and climb the hills and never give up.

UNLESS YOU ARE

FEARLESS

NOTHING WILL CHANGE

Remember to stop and smell
the roses and plant a few
while you are out there.

I had my Big Girl Panties Up the Whole Time

It's a strange title for this chapter. But the truth behind it is so true. My whole life I thought I had to amount to something. I thought I had to live up to an expectation. I worked so hard to get people to like me. I stressed what people thought of me. The lights are turned on and my eyes are open, but what am I seeing.

A vision of what life should be. I used to think I needed to look a certain way. I needed to be smarter. I always felt like I never measured up. But what or who am I measuring up to?

As I got older, I started to know the value of my heartbeat and the strength found in love and friendships.

Love and marriage become about truth and real connections instead of a made-up idea of what marriage should look like.

Have fun in your marriage! It's ok to laugh with each other. Know the hard times will be hard but get through it together. Motherhood is in a class of its own. You learn a lot about life and yourself when you are a mom. You grow with your kids. Your love for them grows as you watch them grow up. To watch them achieve so much because you simply believed in them.

You do not know the future only God does and during your life you might be handed a few trials you were not expecting.

Hold on tight through the storm and do not give up. Let go of what you cannot hold on to. Know that your kids are going to fail too, just like you did, but never give up on them and always love them no matter what. It is through unconditional love that can bring them back.

Here is another poem I wrote. It is about being set free to be who you are meant to be. Give yourself permission to fail so you can learn from it and grow. So, by giving yourself this, let your kids have it too.

Release me, be set free.
Dream who you were meant to be.
Release the doubt and let it all out.
Fearless in it all, you were meant to stand tall.
Open your eyes let beauty be seen
For you have been given the gift most people
dream. Live beyond your measures
Life will bring you treasure
Speak your heart. Let out your soul.
Let me remind you who gave his all.
Follow your path and don't look back.
Hope for tomorrow
But stand firm in today
That you are held in the arms of grace.
Give back and restore a smile
Let them know they are not alone in their trial.
Tragedy can be reversed
Break the curse
Beauty of the soul
Can make us whole.

My big girl panties were up the whole time. I found out how to be me. I did this by simply believing in myself and trust in Gods plan for my life.

Philippians 4:13

I can do all things through Christ who strengthens me.

Your whole life God is working through you and in you to be the best you. If we started out in life with-it all-in front of us, then we would have nowhere to go. Our purpose every morning to get out of bed would be small and there would be no point in a God or Jesus and his sacrifice.

God knows we need to grow our faith. That faith does not appear out of nowhere. Through our trials and the sadness and grief we experience in our life, faith shows up. With our joy and accomplishments faith is expressed and shared with others.

Your faith was there the whole time; you just needed life to pull it out. Most important balance it all. We get short with people, become mad and distant from the most important people in our lives. It is easy to lose focus on what is important. Hold onto your big girl panties during this time in your life. Balance your life. Your time is crucial. Don't let it swallow you and drown you. We each pull up our panties one leg at a time, if they go up, I think you are on the right track.

My purpose and mission for writing this
book is to know.

I will fail and that is ok.

I will fall and I will get back up.

**I don't have too always be
perfect,**

**I know my Big Girl Panties will
fall down.**

**But I will lean over and pull
them right back up.**

I hope you have enjoyed my journey throughout this book and the road I am on is not finished, it is still moving. The lessons keep coming and so does the growth.

This book is dedicated to my twin sister Jennifer. Your life inspires me every day. The time you had on this earth was too short but lived well. You lived beyond what was expected and you loved more people than I can count. Thank you for being my sister and showing me how to be **FEARLESS!**

INDEX

Philippians 4:13

To order this book and more
books written by

Beth Ann Stockton

go to Amazon.

Fearlessenterprise.weeblysite.com

Zack's
First Day of School

#FEARLESSENTERPRISE

Live Like It Matters
and
Love Like Crazy

Beth Ann Stockton

LIFE
SPEAKS
TRUTH

Poetry by
Beth Ann Stockton

I Thought I Pulled Up My BIG

Girl Panties but Apparently

They Fell Down

Made in the USA
Middletown, DE
03 February 2025